THE ENGLISH PLEASURE GARDEN 1660–1860

Sarah Jane Downing

SHIRE PUBLICATIONS

Published in Great Britain in 2013 by Shire Publications Ltd,
PO Box 883, Oxford OX1 9PL, United Kingdom.
PO Box 3985, New York, NY 10185-3983, USA.

E-mail: shire@shirebooks.co.uk   www.shirebooks.co.uk

A CIP catalogue record for this book is available from the
British Library.

Shire Library no. 478   .   ISBN-13: 978 0 74780 699 8

Sarah Jane Downing has asserted her right under the
Copyright, Designs and Patents Act, 1988, to be identified
as the author of this book.

Designed by Ken Vail Graphic Design, Cambridge, UK and
typeset in Perpetua and Gill Sans.
Printed in China through Worldprint Ltd.

13 14 15 16 17   13 12 11 10 9 8 7 6 5 4

COVER IMAGE

The Chinese House, the Rotunda, and the Company in
Masquerade at Ranelagh Gardens.

TITLE PAGE IMAGE

A Tea Garden (1790) by F. D. Soiron after George Morland.
Even the rural idyll of the tea garden was a great
opportunity to display the finest of fashions.

CONTENTS PAGE IMAGE

Fan view of a Georgian Pleasure Garden, possibly Ranelagh.

ACKNOWLEDGEMENTS

My most grateful thanks to David Coke for his support and
generous loan of images from his private collection, pages
18, 24 (top), 35 (bottom), and 55 (top). To Daniel Brown at
Bath In Time (www.bathintime.co.uk) for his kindness and
the loan of his beautiful images of Bath, pages 3, 39, 42, 43
(top), 47 (bottom), and 48 (top). To Olivia Rickman at The
Foundling Museum who has been wonderfully encouraging
and kind in the loan of the image on page 22 (bottom).

I also owe a huge debt of thanks to Norma Watt, Assistant
Keeper of Art at Norwich Castle Museum & Art Gallery, for
use of the image on page 40; to Tom Heaven at Birmingham
Museums and Art Galleries for searching, rediscovering, and
photographing the painting of Vauxhall Gardens at
Duddeston, page 45 for me; to Compton Verney for the
wonderful Canalettos on page 6 (top) and page 28; to Roger
Hull from Liverpool Record Office, page 44; to Cristoph
Bull from Gravesend Library, page 60; the V&A, page
21(top); and Bridgeman Art Library/Private Collection,
page 6 (top), Private Collection/Photo © Christie's
Images/The Bridgeman Art Library, page 28, and
Bridgeman Art Library/© Museum of London, page 54.

Except for Bath, information about the provincial Pleasure
Gardens is extremely scarce, and I offer my utmost
appreciation to those super people who helped me find it:
Kath Lapsley from Manchester Archives and Local Studies,
Lisa Brown at Boston Library Cultural Services, Norma
Hampson of Warwickshire Gardens Trust, Jayne Rounce of
Little Owl Books for sharing her copy of *Newcastle Upon Tyne:
Its Growth and Achievement* with me, and to Philip Norman at
the Museum of Garden History for his wonderful insight
into horticultural history.

Finally my heartfelt thanks to Emma, Sacha, my father, and
especially my mother for her French and Latin translations,
and to those fabulous people at Shire Publications, Nick
Wright, Sarah Hodder, and Russell Butcher.

Shire Publications is supporting the Woodland Trust, the UK's leading woodland conservation charity, by funding the dedication of trees.

CONTENTS

INTRODUCTION

THE STORY of the Pleasure Gardens takes in almost three centuries, from before the Great Fire devastated London to the height of Victoria's reign. In our century we have diversified the venues for our entertainment, with hundreds of places competing to fulfil our needs, but in the days when leisure was scarce – when a holiday was really only a day – the Pleasure Gardens offered all that could be dreamt of.

The English Civil War and the revolutions that followed – Jacobite, American, French and Industrial – brought the beginning of the modern age, but in so doing they also destroyed the old order. If politics could challenge sovereignty and science could challenge religion, what could be relied upon? The only thing seemingly unchanging was nature, and even that was being used and perceived in new ways as medicine switched from a female vocation to a male profession, the class system evolved and the economy shifted to trade rather than agriculture.

At the Restoration, the King returned with a European education and erudite tastes that allowed pleasure to be connected with culture. England was delighted, especially the nobility, and a line was drawn under the philistinism and austerity of the interregnum. The theatres were revived; the first public concert was performed in 1672; society reconnected with the imperative to heal the rifts of the Civil War; and, with relief, suspicions were suspended to allow for a new era of tolerance.

Ideas of civilisation and control were reviewed in the light of Jean Jacques Rousseau's 'noble savage' – the concept that constraints of society would corrupt man's inherent goodness – which influenced all manner of issues, including concepts of childcare, the call for the abolition of slavery, and the abandonment of the formal garden. It was the age of Enlightenment and for the first time a gentleman needed to demonstrate his education. Wealth was well enough, but without the elegant taste derived from a classical education it was no longer a true indicator of noble status, and taking the Grand Tour became an essential rite of passage.

Opposite:
The magical glittering beauty of the Grand Orchestra at Vauxhall Pleasure Gardens (1803).

5

The Grand Walk, Vauxhall Gardens by Giovanni Antonio Canal (1751). Whilst living in England from 1746–55 Canaletto painted its most glorious sights, including Vauxhall Gardens – his painting was seen throughout Europe and inspired many imitators including Tivoli Gardens in Copenhagen.

Bacchus and Ariadne by Titian (1520–3). The Classical and Romantic subject was typical of those seen on the Grand Tour, which came to influence the Arcadian dreams of the Enlightenment and became a popular subject at the Pleasure Gardens.

London was not just the Court, but the city as defined by the social season and its round of plays, concerts and events. Whilst gentlemen were at their clubs and coffee houses, upper-class women found time on their hands to shop and beautify, and fashions flourished to the fullest extent of decadent imagination. As in our own age, to be celebrated as a lady or gentleman of fashion was the social pinnacle, and one of the greatest pleasures was 'to see and be seen' – especially if one found oneself in the same company as royalty.

It was an increasingly visual age, with an element of theatricality applied wholesale, from the spectacular costumes created for the ever-popular masquerade to the aura of mystery cultivated by the highwayman. The fashionable spaces such as the Pantheon were decorated with vivid scenes and adorned with multiple mirrors that allowed many fleeting encounters with oneself. The Pleasure Gardens excelled in *trompe l'œil* scenes and artworks frequently created by artists with a theatrical background, and they quite literally put the fashionable in the limelight, with a wealth of lamps glittering in the night.

The ever-expanding city also had disadvantages. Although the new architecture was an exaltation of spacious elegance, much of the old city was a rat run of dirty, overcrowded alleys. Night soil rained down into the stream of sewerage that washed along the centre of most streets, pushed along by the flocks of animals, coaches and sedans. Rarely was there a dedicated sidewalk, and road surfacing was either muddy squelch or treacherous, uneven cobbles. There was also the ever-present risk of robbery by highwaymen or pickpockets, only partly alleviated by the advent of the Fielding brothers' Bow Street court. These hazards, not to mention the pungent odours, were hardly conducive to taking a pleasant stroll, and yet walking was the preferred form of exercise for the fashionable, giving ample opportunity for display.

The horror of the plague still haunted with each periodic visit until 1665, and the pox in various varieties ravaged rich and poor alike. Good health was keenly sought at any costs, and the spas such as Epsom became fashionable from the 1630s, serving their bitter mineral waters as a panacea. Although they were eagerly drunk to cure everything from infertility to worms, it was largely a health cure for the healthy, taken more for the society than anything

Above left:
Getting Into the Coach. After the dour restraint of the Puritan era, people couldn't wait to put on their sometimes amazing finery and enjoy the new entertainments.

Above right:
The Pit Ticket by Hogarth. Cockfighting was a popular pastime for all classes of men who liked to gamble. With 'entertainments' like this, the Pleasure Gardens must have been a most welcome antidote.

Above: Lady Betty Bustle dressing for the Pantheon, her elaborate dress complemented by a black silk full face mask or complexion preserver, the dim candlelight of her room in dramatic contrast to the glittering lights of her destination.

Above right: Sedan chairs were a convenient way to beat the traffic and avoid pickpockets. There was no need to risk the dirt or weather, as the chairmen would convey passengers from entrance hall to entrance hall.

else. A Cavalier custom acquired in Europe, the spa indulged romance in both senses and provided a welcome antidote to the sobriety of the city.

All of these elements conspired to create the Pleasure Gardens. The air was clean and perfumed; the manicured walks were luxurious to walk upon, allowing voluminous skirts and dainty high heels to remain clean; and the romance of sun-dappled bowers allowed heads to spin. By the mid eighteenth century there were more than sixty Pleasure Gardens within the London area, with many others throughout England usually to be found in larger towns or spa towns.

Divided broadly into three types, the first form was primarily bowling greens at pubs or tea gardens, offering pleasant space (but limited social opportunity) to those who wished to play the game made popular in

A private coach was an important status symbol, especially a 'glass coach' with windows, costing more than a middle-class person's yearly salary. A Countess would display her rank with a bare-headed coachman – preferably with a gleaming bald pate.

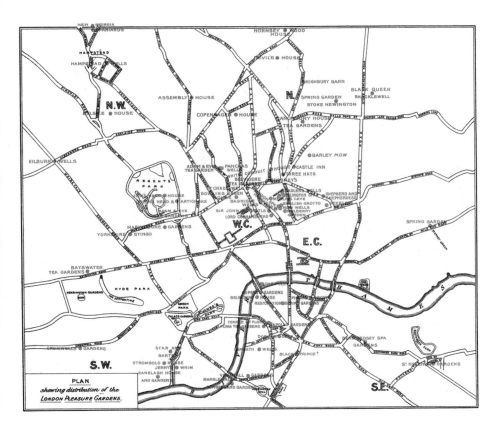

Shakespeare's day. The second variety of Pleasure Garden also favoured bowls: it was recommended exercise at the spas, as was walking, and these fashionable resorts often divided their more attractive spaces with gravelled walks. They frequently gave a greater variety of entertainments and cuisine – presumably as antidote to the brackish waters – and that eighteenth-century delight, the public breakfast. Finally, the third form was that of the great Pleasure Gardens such as those at Vauxhall and Ranelagh, which seemed like a fairytale dream. These offered new realms of decadence, an Arcadia on earth, where fantastical sights glimpsed in variegated light through gilded foliage summoned the glamours of the ancient gods whose dominion was the forest, whose currency was pleasure.

Sadly, not all the Pleasure Gardens can make an appearance here, only a selection to represent the three main forms as they existed in London and the provinces, charting their evolution from pretty rustic idyll in the seventeenth century, through the Rococo splendour of the eighteenth century, to the gaudy family fun of the Victorian era.

Plan showing the distribution of the sixty-four London Pleasure Gardens in existence during the eighteenth century.

9

THE FIRST GARDENS

T HE SEVENTEENTH CENTURY was dominated by the Civil War and its long-term ramifications, not least the massive destruction that saw the face of England irrevocably changed. Although Cromwell was fond of Spring Gardens and its bowling green at Charing Cross in London – one of the very first Pleasure Gardens surviving from the days of Charles I – his appreciation of the sylvan landscape did not stop him from allowing his troops to scythe down great swathes of forest to fuel his war machine. Even individual estates were de-beautified as Puritan thought decreed that a garden should be a place for contemplation of Christ's suffering, and that a garden of flowers was a 'garden of vanities'.

By the end of the seventeenth century, inspired by the beauties of Versailles, Hampton Court, Longleat and Chatsworth, the garden evoked not only status, but fashion. With the Restoration came a sense of prosperity and permanence, and many landowners wanted to improve their properties. Where many had updated their knot gardens with larger, simpler quincunxes – squares or rectangles of grass framed with gravel paths, punctuated at corners and focal points with statues, exotic potted plants or topiary – designers such as London and Wise were leading the way with majestic sweeping hedges and rich ostentatious design. Both themes showed their influence in the Pleasure Gardens that were gradually to spring up across the country, as the garden had become the essential setting for English life, and increasingly English social life.

NEW SPRING GARDENS (1661)
In the fragrant summer of 1661 the New Spring Gardens were opened on the Lambeth side of the river Thames: these were the genuinely pastoral roots of the Pleasure Garden that was to become one of the most glorious sights of eighteenth-century London – Vauxhall Pleasure Gardens.

There are few references to the gardens before the beginning of the eighteenth century. Probably the first is made by John Evelyn in his diary for 2 July 1661, when he records it as 'a prettily contrived plantation'.

Opposite:
Arriving by water made the most stylish entrance to Cuper's Gardens, the boats moored Venetian-style. During the 1740s, Cuper's became known for its elaborate firework displays, attracting fashionable and even royal patronage from the Prince and Princess of Wales.

It seems no views
of New Spring
Gardens remain
from the
seventeenth
century. The first
reliable view was
in blue and white
on Pinchbeck's
Vauxhall Fan
(1736), which
probably inspired
this view by
George Besant.

Samuel Pepys echoes his sentiment in his own diary entry for 29 May 1662, when he compares it most favourably with the Old Spring Garden – another public garden, which occupied an adjacent spot until the late 1660s:

'To the Old Spring Garden, and there walked long, and the wenches gathered pinks. Here we staid, and seeing that we could not have anything to eat, but very dear, and with long stay, we went forth again without any notice taken of us... Thence to the New one, where I never was before, which much exceeds the other ... and here we had cakes and powdered beef and ale, and so home again by water with much pleasure.'

*The Pleasures of
Life.* It is thought
that the man
seated is intended
to be Frederick,
Prince of Wales.
His Royal Pavilion
is shown in the
background along
with the orchestra.

The Invitation to Mira, featuring Louis François Roubiliac's statue of Handel as Apollo with his lyre and Pegasus behind. It was published in June 1738, a month after the unveiling of the celebrated statue that was a major feature during Tyers's reign.

Below: The Farewell to Vaux Hall. With his song, Sam Godwin captured the sentiment at the end of the immensely successful opening season of 1732: that no one wanted to see it close for the winter.

The New Spring Gardens relied largely upon nature's glories: from the flowers and cherries (which could be eaten from the trees) to the music of birdsong; but cheesecakes, syllabubs, viands and ale were also served from the Master's House. Monsieur de Monconys describes it in a journal of his visit to England in 1663, admiring it for 'its lawns and the "politeness" of its sanded walks bordered with hedges of gooseberries and rosebushes'.

The property that, under Jonathan Tyers, eventually became the famous Vauxhall Pleasure Gardens was known up until the end of the seventeenth century variously as Fox Hall, Faulkes Hall and New Spring Gardens, the name which persisted in tandem with Vaux Hall until the mid eighteenth century. The 'spring' in question was not named for the season, but rather for the concealed jets of water that, as at Versailles, would surprise unsuspecting promenaders who triggered the sprays inadvertently, much to the hilarity of the dry onlookers.

Pepys recalls music in the gardens in 1667 from a harp, fiddles and a Jew's trump, but he also notes the appearance of young gallants misbehaving, breaching supper boxes uninvited and insulting the ladies. As distressing as this rowdy behaviour may have been for some, it also added a frisson of illicit excitement for others. As Tom Brown, writing of the darker walks of the garden, notes in his *Amusements* of 1700: 'both

The joyful romantic music of the nightingale was one of the great delights of the early Pleasure Gardens.

sexes meet, and mutually serve one another as guides to lose their way, and the windings and turnings in the little Wildernesses are so intricate, that the most experienced mothers have often lost themselves in looking for their daughters'.

All this fuelled the endless cycle of gossip that was society's sustenance, as Vanbrugh's Lady Fanciful states in *The Provoked Wife*: ''tis infallibly some intrigue that brings them to Spring Garden'.

This suggestion that the garden was used for secret or unsavoury assignations is hinted at by a somewhat hypocritical Pepys who dines with Mrs Knipp there – 'it being darkish' – and is confirmed in Joseph Addison's account of his visit in 1712, by which time it appears to have slipped into ill repute: 'As we were going out of the Garden, my old Friend, told the Mistress of the House, who sat at the Bar, That he should be a better Customer to her Garden, if there were more Nightingales, and fewer Strumpets.'

OTHER SEVENTEENTH-CENTURY GARDENS

Vauxhall was not the only Pleasure Garden that saw its origins in the unrest of the seventeenth century. Seeking to provide a sanctuary more than entertainment, the early gardens in London offered a beautiful, peaceful haven from the threat of 'plague humors' – providing a sweet-smelling contrast to the city, which, in the days before the Great Fire, was a teeming warren of filth within the old city walls. Sometimes, as at Islington Spa (1684–1840) and Pancras Wells (1697–*c.*1795), a long or 'Great' room was available for dancing in the morning or afternoon, and quiet booths were

Above:
The Folly on the Thames. Nearby at Waterloo Bridge was the 'Folly', looking like a floating castle topped by four turrets. From c.1668 to 1720 it offered music and dancing, burnt brandy and private booths, but was notorious as a rendezvous for 'ladies of the town'.

Right:
There was an attempt to rename the 'Folly' as the 'Royal Diversion' after Queen Mary visited, but the gambling and scandalous reputation remained until in its final years it became popular with shop workers who would row up the Thames after work.

Below:
Sadler's Wells initially used the epithet of 'New Tunbridge Wells' when it opened in the 1680s, much to the consternation of the Kentish original, which published a tract decrying their waters, their Islington air and their diversions.

provided for playing the fashionable card games or gambling. Cuper's Gardens was opened in 1691; it boasted good bowling greens and a classical ambience, created by the Arundel Marbles. Rescued from the demolition of Arundel House in The Strand, the mutilated remains of the ancient statuary were distributed throughout the gardens.

More than a century before the ballet of the same name was founded, Sadler's Wells offered a little more. When Sadler was building a music house in the gardens at his inn in 1683, workmen uncovered an intricately carved ancient well. Suspecting that the water might have medicinal qualities to rival the already popular Tunbridge Wells, he had it tested, then added extended formal gardens surrounding an ornamental marble basin. He also had the foresight to appoint tumblers and rope dancers to entertain visitors to the gardens along with an open air bandstand 'on a rock and shell construction' for dancing.

Spinacuti's monkey was the highlight of the 1768 season at Sadler's Wells, with his dazzling tightrope feats – a kind of simian forerunner to Blondin!

MARYLEBONE GARDENS (1650)

Marylebone Gardens became a pleasure resort in 1650 when the gardens were separated from Marylebone Manor House, which was once a hunting

lodge belonging to Henry VIII. There was a
bowling green that could be accessed by the Rose
Tavern or the Rose of Normandie Tavern on
Marylebone High Street, but it wasn't until 1738
that they became Pleasure Gardens in the full
sense. It was at that point that they also started to
charge an entrance fee: 12 shillings bought a
season ticket for two, or sixpence each on the
gate, the charge to be offset against refreshments.

In 1659, as well as the bowling green, the
gardens had a circular walk and gravel walks
'double set with quick set hedges, full grown and
indented like town walls' all encircled with a
brick wall and fruit trees. Pepys found it to be
pretty when he visited on 7 May 1668, and in its
incarnation in the 1690s as Long's Bowling
Green, it attracted a select clientele of 'quality'.
By the time of Queen Anne it was also notorious
as a gambling house where the Duke of
Buckingham held his end of season dinner to the

toast: 'May as many of us as remain unhanged next spring meet here again.'
It was also immortalised in the *Beggar's Opera* (1728) as the favoured haunt of
the highwayman Macheath.

MY LORD'S GARDEN (1663)

Norwich, which was one of England's prosperous principal towns in the
seventeenth century, was also fond of its gardens. The first Pleasure Garden
outside London that was not dedicated to a spa, My Lord's Garden was
designed and created by Henry Howard, brother to Thomas, Duke of
Norfolk. Evelyn had noted the abundance of fine flower gardens in Norwich
so it may be that inspiration was local. The first reference came in a journal
entry for 1 January 1664:

> 'By the water side in Cunsford which hee [Howard] intends for a place of
> recreation, having made already walkes round and crosse it, forty foot in
> bredth; if the quadrangle left be spatious enough hee intends the first of them
> for a bowling green, the third for a wildernesse, and the forth for a [flower]
> garden.'

May Day at
London Spa (1720).
A popular resort
for milkmaids and
their swain, it was
renowned for its
chalybeate spring
and the fine ale it
made – where,
unusually, the poor
were given the
water for free.

STOLEN MOMENTS
AND HALCYON DAYS

THE PLEASURE GARDENS of the eighteenth century provided a cornucopia of entertainments from dinner and dancing to promenading and gossip. Even the trip over the water necessary to reach Vauxhall, Cuper's and various other gardens offered a symbolic escape to the exotic. A visit to the gardens presented for the first time a respectable pursuit that was open to everyone who could afford the entrance fee, rather than by invitation according to title and class. Princesses, ladies, debutantes and courtesans paraded in the latest fashions advertising their beauty, as being seen at Ranelagh and Vauxhall in particular became a vital part of 'the season'. Everybody who was anybody partook of the pleasures of the gardens from Pepys to Walpole, the Pitts Elder and Younger, John Wesley (the founder of Methodism), Admiral Nelson and Dick Turpin.

With such stars as Capability Brown and Humphrey Repton, the eighteenth century is often regarded as the heyday of English gardening. The 'landscape' style was a delicate harmony of nature and nurture: the use of judicious artifice allowed vast acres of countryside to appear utterly natural and unspoilt. Whilst the concealed ditches of ha-has provided invisible control for the livestock, a distant classical temple could infer an 'ancient' connection to the land even if there wasn't one and allusions to that increasingly fashionable gentlemanly rite of passage, the Grand Tour.

This blend of fashion, wealth and fervent social posturing was also essential to the Pleasure Gardens, which provided the same classical foil and glamorous associations in carefully contrived 'natural' scenery – with just a frisson of Bacchanalian debauchery.

VAUXHALL GARDENS (1728–67)
Although the New Spring Gardens was casual and natural in its beauty, which paraded unfettered in a riot of colour surrounding the sanded walks, when Jonathan Tyers took it over, establishing it as Vauxhall Gardens in 1728, he had a stronger vision. Inspired by Milton's *Masque of Comus*, first performed at Ludlow Castle in 1634, Tyers created a sophisticated vision of Arcadian beauty to appeal to the most romantic sensibilities.

Opposite:
The Triumphal Arches (courtesy of David Coke). The ornate triumphal arches led the eye to a painting of the ruins of Palmyra at the eastern end. For many years the semicircular sweep of pavilions provided a backdrop for Roubiliac's statue of Handel.

Right:
The Temple of Comus was a wonderfully exotic setting for the evening's romantic revelries, the striking architecture creating a huge impact fifty years before the Brighton Pavilion. Each supper box was the perfect frame, displaying the fashionable visitors whilst they 'people-watched'.

Far right:
The Rococo Comus as he appeared in Garrick's production in 1752.

The story of Comus, the son of Circe and Bacchus, summons perfectly the conflicted human desires that fuelled the Romantic Movement. Comus is a Pan-like creature of the secret decadence of the night, attempting to ply virtuous young ladies with his 'orient liquor' and introduce them to the pleasures of the flesh and nature. In celebration Tyers built the Temple of Comus, and with a hint of irony he created the perfect metaphor, as the elegant social parade that strolled through the pavilions and the music room contrasted with the secret places along the dark walks.

After extensive remodelling, New Spring Gardens was opened for the first time as Vauxhall Gardens, with a fabulous *Ridotto Al Fresco* on Wednesday 7 June 1732 offering a hint of the delights that were to come. Legend has it that Tyers was in suicidal despair until the artist William Hogarth suggested the idea for such a grand opening along with a series of paintings for the supper boxes to be created by Francis Hayman and artists from Hogarth's St Martin's Lane Academy. The opening night was attended by four hundred guests (who arrived at 9 pm and stayed until 3 am); obviously far more were anticipated, as a hundred armed soldiers with bayonets fixed were on hand as security. The majority of the company, which included Prince Frederick, were beautifully decorous in formal Lawyers' gowns and Domino cloaks, but there were a couple of infractions when a drunken waiter donned masquerade dress and a pickpocket was caught stealing 50 guineas.

Many misconceptions were held about the Vauxhall supper box paintings and often images of them have been reproduced in reverse.

Above: *The Milkmaid's Garland With Its Usual Attendants* or *Humours of May Day* (1741–2) by Francis Hayman (courtesy of the V&A). Hayman created idyllic playful pastoral scenes for many of the boxes, including this view of the London milkmaids' traditional May Day dance garlanded with flowers and ribbons beneath mountains of borrowed silver.

Below, from left to right:

Building Houses With Cards, supper box painting by Francis Hayman with the engraver Hubert François Gravelot. It is possible that a young Gainsborough contributed the central seated figure whilst he was studying under Hayman.

The Wapping Landlady and the Tars Who Are Just Come Ashore by Hayman. Only a fragment of this supper box painting remains, showing the two seated figures – many of the paintings were greeted and handled with such enthusiasm that they were severely damaged or destroyed.

Mademoiselle Catherina the Famous Dwarf by Hayman, displayed in a supper box on the south side of the Grove. Mademoiselle Catherina was in this instance a dancing automaton displayed by a trio of Savoyards, one playing a hurdy-gurdy.

The Devil To Pay, a supper box scene by Hayman from the popular 1731 ballad opera by Charles Coffey. Along with triumphant military views in the Rotunda, he painted scenes from literature, including various selections from Shakespeare displayed in the Prince's Pavilion.

Prince Frederick became such a regular visitor that Tyers built him the Prince of Wales Pavilion set at the western end of the gardens facing the orchestra, with a private room behind and a concealed entrance to the street. He continued to attend throughout his life, bringing a coterie of 'beautiful people' who would have attracted a host of far more humble citizens just as today's celebrities do. Vauxhall was never truly exclusive, allowing admittance to all those who could afford the entrance fee of a shilling per evening, except for masquerade nights.

Before Westminster Bridge was built the visitors to Vauxhall arrived by water, some taking great delight in the journey, such as Miss Lydia Welford, who exclaims within the pages of Tobias Smollett's *The Expedition of Humphrey Clinker* (1771) that: 'At nine o'clock, in a charming moonlight evening, we embarked at Ranelagh for Vauxhall, in a wherry so light and slender that we looked like so many fairies sailing in a nutshell.' Unfortunately the greeting at Vauxhall was far less magical, where 'there was a terrible confusion of wherries and a crowd of people bawling, and swearing, and quarrelling.'

Once safely ashore visitors paid their entrance shilling or showed their silver passes at the gate adjacent to the Manager's House at the western end of the gardens. They then passed through a dark passage to burst into the amazing glittering gardens, supplied by over 1,000 oil lamps strung within and between the lofty trees.

Famille rose punch bowl with oval foliate panel depicting the Grand Walk, Vauxhall Gardens in the 1750s on one side, with a view of the Foundling Hospital, on the other, *Qianlong, c.* 1790 (Courtesy of The Foundling Museum) Vauxhall's irrepressible fame was proliferated by the various prints and objects that bore its image, which in turn became more fashionable by association.

The South Walk and the Dark Walk. The South Walk ran east, parallel to the Grand Walk, through three triumphal arches. The Lovers' or Druid's Walk, known popularly as the Dark Walk, also ran parallel from behind the pavilions.

From the main entrance the Grand Walk, lined with elm trees, led away more than 900 feet to a gilded statue of Aurora and the eastern perimeter fence, beyond which meadow land swept away into the distance. Running parallel was the South Walk, also lined with trees; it was traversed by three triumphal arches, which as you walked east framed your view of a painting of the ruins of Palmyra. The Grand Cross Walk passed across the gardens at right angles, entering the Lovers' or Druid's walk at the right, where there was another painted scene of an artistic ruin, and the Wilderness and Rural Downs to the left. These 'dark walks' were home to a host of nightingales, blackbirds and thrushes who provided a serenade to rival the orchestra.

(a) The gold ticket presented to Hogarth by Jonathan Tyers in return for his help – inscribed 'In perpetuam beneficii memoriam', offering complimentary entrance for him and 'a coach' of up to five guests for life. The ticket was still in use in the 1840s. (b) Silver season ticket depicting the gardens' celebrated attraction, Roubiliac's statue of Handel as Apollo/Orpheus, with exergue stating 'BLANDIUS ORPHEO' – 'enticing Orpheus'. Season tickets would admit two; the price for the 1732 season was 1 guinea, rising to 2 guineas in 1748. (c) Silver season ticket featuring Amphion on a dolphin, probably designed by Hogarth. Amphion was the King of Thebes; he played a lyre with such power and skill that boulders and rocks would move and change shape thus creating architecture. (d) Silver season ticket 'Summer', probably designed by Hogarth – it would be prudent to invoke the goddess of summer in the hope of ensuring fine weather! She is depicted with Cupid flying with a scroll reading 'Frondosa Reducitur Aestas' – 'leafy summer is brought back'. (e) Silver season ticket for Mr Carey featuring the ancient Greek goddess Thalia, probably designed by Hogarth. Thalia was the Muse of comedy and one of the Graces closely associated with Apollo – she was the personification of the sun's rays bringing flowers and fruitfulness.

Dr Syntax at Vauxhall Gardens (courtesy of David Coke). Rowlandson's satirical character holds up a slice of the notoriously stingy ham to show that the candlelight could shine right through it! One of Vauxhall's chefs once boasted that he could slice it so thinly that he could cover the entire 12 acres with the meat from just one ham.

Thomas Lowe, proprietor of Marylebone Gardens (1763–8). He placed the emphasis of the entertainments on concerts mainly featuring himself, but sadly his business acumen did not match his vocal talents.

They were so beloved that rumour has it that when building work drove these 'feathered minstrels' away one season, Tyers hired people to hide within the shrubbery imitating the birdsong.

The grassy Rural Downs were covered with cypresses, firs and cedars, where Milton sat listening to the music – at least in leaden statue form illuminated by lamps. Soft, mysterious fairy music also haunted this place from the 'musical bushes' supplied by a 'subterranean orchestra'. The technology used isn't clear but by the mid eighteenth century it was over, 'the natural damp of the earth being found prejudicial to the instruments'.

Approximately five of the twelve acres formed the Grove, a quadrangle framed by the Grand Walk, the Cross Walk and the South Walk, with the Orchestra in the centre facing the Master's House and the Prince of Wales Pavilion at the western end. The Rotunda music room was also at this end with the Grand Pavilion; the other supper boxes and pavilions swept in gracious curves towards the end of the Grove, with a few more flanked by benches crossing the end behind the Orchestra.

Vauxhall was a magnum opus for Tyers, and shortly before his death on 1 July 1767 he asked to be carried into the Grove so that he could take a last look and say a fond farewell.

MARYLEBONE GARDENS (1736–68)

The eighteenth century brought entertainments beyond gambling and bowling to Marylebone Gardens. In 1718 there was a special concert with fireworks to celebrate the birthday of King George I, but the entertainment programme didn't begin in earnest until 1736, when a tower of scaffolding was erected for the Flying Man who walked a high wire with a wheelbarrow. By 1740 the proprietor Daniel Gough had styled it as a place of evening entertainments. He built an elegant Garden Orchestra with an organ for concerts, and balls and suppers were held in the House, or Great Room. He was superseded

approximately a decade later by John Thursler, a professional chef who, with the help of his daughter and her superb plum and seed cake and almond cheesecakes, made Marylebone Gardens famous for its catering at stylish breakfasts or dinners and for serving coffee, tea or chocolate at any time of day.

Wealthy Londoners kept country homes in Marylebone, but for less privileged visitors the greatest disadvantage to Marylebone Gardens was distance, allowing many opportunities for highwaymen and footpads to strike. In response, a guard of soldiers was on hand to accompany visitors to and from the gardens, escorting them back to town as far as the Foundling Hospital. Despite these efforts made in the early 1740s, Mary-bone fields became a notorious spot, and on 15 June 1763 a pair of footpads provided a different form of popular entertainment when they were hanged at nearby Tyburn for robbing the waiters who worked at the gardens. This prompted the proprietors in 1764 to offer 'a premium of ten guineas' to anyone who could apprehend a highwayman or footpad on the road to the gardens.

Above left: Handel frequently visited the gardens, which became famous for their performances, often of Handel's own works.

Above right: George Cruickshank's illustration of Marylebone Gardens for Ainsworth's novel *The Miser's Daughter* (1842).

Marylebone from Wigmore Street in 1750, described by Cowper: 'Suburban villas, highway-side retreats, That dread th'encroachment of our growing streets, Tight boxes, neatly sash'd, and in a blaze With all a July sun's collected rays, Delight the citizen, who, gasping there, Breathes clouds of dust, and calls it country air.'

RANELAGH: THE DIVINEST PLACE UNDER HEAVEN

A LTHOUGH VAUXHALL shared London's social scene with more than sixty lesser spas, tea gardens and resorts, it was only the advent of Ranelagh in 1742 that offered serious competition. In 1733 the former home of the Earl of Ranelagh was earmarked for development as a pleasure resort by Lacey, the Patentee of the Drury Lane Theatre, but opposition from the nearby Royal Hospital stayed progress until 1741, when work began on the great rotunda or, as it was initially called, Amphitheatre, designed by East India Company architect William Jones.

Built as an echo to the rotunda at the Pantheon in Rome, Ranelagh's rotunda spanned a huge 150 feet. Its walls were 17 feet thick supporting a vast domed ceiling painted olive, bordered by a rainbow from which hung numerous gilt and crystal chandeliers ablaze with candles. The magnificent central structure, its marbled columns surmounted by gilded caryatids, originally contained the orchestra, but disadvantageous acoustics caused it to be moved to the side. The centrepiece became a huge fireplace, its warmth allowing Ranelagh to offer refuge on the typically damp and chilly summer evenings and to offer entertainments for a longer season, often beginning in February, whereas the others waited until Easter. The 555-foot circumference held fifty-two supper boxes, each able to accommodate a party of eight, decorated with a 'droll painting' and bell lamp with candles. A similar number were on the upper balcony, accessed by sliding doors from the gallery that ran around the upper floor outside.

A 1793 guidebook lists 'walking round the rotundo as one of the pleasures of the place' and much was said of 'the circular labour' – although not always favourably. Walpole, as the satirical 'Harlequin in Ranelagh' in *London* magazine (1774), named it 'the ring of folly'.

Whilst Vauxhall could boast of its transparently thin ham, and Marylebone of its delicious confectionery, Ranelagh served 'regales' of tea or coffee with bread and butter included with the admission price of half a crown. In the early years before 1754, admission was as little as a couple of shillings to include the extremely popular public breakfast concert at noon.

Opposite:
The Great Walk ran parallel to the canal, beyond which were the formal gardens and, according to the *Perspective Plan of the Rotunda and Gardens 1745*, 'boxes for gentlemen to smoak in'.

Evening concerts began in May 1742; the music within the rotunda could be punctuated by walking in the gardens between acts. There were several gravel walks lined by elms and yews, the principal walk going from Ranelagh house to the circular Temple of Pan at the bottom of the gardens. The lamps that glittered amongst the trees trailed shimmering reflections in the canal, surmounted by a temple that was known both as the Chinese House and the Venetian Temple.

FASHION

Ranelagh was considered the height of fashion, as two maids argue in the play *High Life Below Stairs* (1759):

> Lady Charlotte's Maid: Well I say it again, I love Vauxhall.
> Lady Bab's Maid: Oh my stars! Why, there is nobody there but filthy citizens
> — Runnelow for my money.

Ranelagh also set its own fashions, as by the 1770s silver Ranelagh silks and Ranelagh waistcoats in silver, gold or other colours were being advertised. The *Percy Anecdotes of Fashion* (1822) recalls the Ranelagh Mob Cap as a fashion in 1762. It was introduced by Mrs Jane Douglas, a lady 'of rather questionable

Ranelagh: Interior of The Rotunda by Giovanni Antonio Canaletto, 1754 (courtesy of Bridgeman Art Library). Constable said that Canaletto 'saw England through Venetian eyes', and the rich formal elegance of the Rotunda was never captured so vividly.

reputation' who lived near Covent Garden and copied the style of headdress from the women of the market there, using a scotch lawn double neck handkerchief. It was folded about the head, crossed under the chin and fastened behind the neck, 'hanging like a pair of pigeons' tails'.

Henry Angelo in his *Reminiscences* declares that Ranelagh was frequented by 'the elite of fashion', the gentlemen wearing powder, frills and ruffles with gold-headed canes; 'cropped heads, trousers, or shoe-strings' would not be countenanced.

THE MASQUERADE

Ranelagh staged some innovative performances, but it was for its lavish masquerade parties that it became best known. The 'Grand Jubilee Masquerade in the Venetian Taste' took place on Wednesday 26 April 1749 in celebration of peace at Aix-La-Chapelle. Horace Walpole described it in a letter a few days later:

> 'It had nothing Venetian in it, but was by far the best understood and prettiest spectacle I ever saw; nothing in a fairy tale ever surpassed it … it began at 3 o'clock; at about five, people of fashion began to go; when you entered, you found the whole garden filled with masks and spread with tents. In one quarter was a maypole dressed with garlands, and people dancing round it to a tabor and pipe, and rustic music, all masked, as were all the various bands of music that were disposed in different parts of the garden; some like huntsmen with French horns, some like peasants, and a troop of harlequins

Above left: George Cruickshank's depiction of dancing in the Rotunda at Ranelagh – the dancing must have been a pleasant change from the ceaseless promenade in the 'circle of folly'!

Above right: *A Man Trap*. Fashion was a vital social tool to proclaim importance in the gardens, where the social strata weren't segregated, and beauty achieved its own status. Contemporary commentators complained that it was too difficult to distinguish a fashionable lady from a courtesan.

George Cruickshank's depiction of the masquerade at Ranelagh Gardens. The spectacular, almost theatrical setting was the perfect backdrop for ever more fantastical costumes sometimes adorned with hundreds of thousands of pounds-worth of jewels.

The morning after the masquerade. The licentiousness that became associated with the masquerade had long caused outrage. Finally it was stated in 1795: 'no amusement seems to have fallen into greater contempt than masquerades. In fact they were never suited to the English – a people naturally sedate and observant of public decency.'

and scaramouches in the little open temple on the mount. On the canal was a sort of gondola adorned with flags and streamers, and filled with music, rowing about. All round the outside of the amphitheatre were shops and all the shopkeepers in mask… There were booths for tea and wine, gaming-tables, and dancing, and about two thousand persons. In short, it pleased me more than the finest thing I ever saw.'

The Jubilee Ridotto in May 1769 unfortunately lived up to the rakish reputation becoming associated with masquerades. The beautiful evening featured floating on the canal 'a large sea-horse stuck full of small lamps', but unfortunately the wine and sweetmeats included in the guinea ticket price were not forthcoming, and a group of gentlemen stormed the wine cellars to serve themselves!

The Ranelagh Regatta and Ball was the event of 1775, converting the Thames into a floating town. Wild estimations of 200,000 or 3 million spectators were recorded as the whole of the river from London Bridge to Millbank teemed with pleasure boats, gambling tables and vendors offering liquor, regatta cards and regatta songs. Cannon fire started the boat race after which the director's barge led the way to Ranelagh, gold regatta ensign flying, the river gleaming, awash with the sparkle of an immense firework display.

Fortunes flagged in the late 1770s, however, and only really revived in 1791 when a programme of masquerades commanded ever more spectacular costumes. A scene of an exploding Mount Etna as at Marylebone twenty years before pleased crowds for a few seasons, but despite a diverse selection of entertainments, Ranelagh finally fell from fashion and served its last regale of tea on 8 July 1803.

Below left: Invitation to Ranelagh May Ball. Ranelagh elevated the masquerade ball to an art form, with a cornucopia of exotic costumes inviting even more extraordinary behaviour, like the notorious appearance of Miss Chudleigh, scandalous in a transparent gown as Iphigenia.

Below: Ticket for the Ranelagh Regatta Ball. The Thames was routinely colonised for the Frost Fair, but for the Regatta Ball it became a floating town of more than 2,000 pleasure boats with countless scaffolds for spectators along the banks, even on top of Westminster Hall.

REGATTA BALL AT RANELAGH
XXIII JUNE MDCCLXXV

Ranelagh Houfe Thursday—May 15 Ball.

The Doors to be opened at nine

MARYLEBONE AND VAUXHALL: THE LATER YEARS

R ANELAGH had changed everything. Although its entertainments were not too different from those at Vauxhall and Marylebone, it was certainly perceived as more exclusive. Bored or not with the circle of eternal folly, as Walpole said, '[Ranelagh] has totally beat Vauxhall. Nobody goes anywhere else', and Vauxhall and Marylebone lost many of their most illustrious visitors.

MARYLEBONE (1760–76)

Several atrociously wet summers at the end of the 1760s prompted the new proprietor, musician Dr Samuel Arnold, to advertise rather unglamorously 'very effectual drains' that would ensure the gardens were 'very dry and pleasant a short time after heavy rains' and a new covered dancing platform.

Fireworks had become a major attraction by 1772 – with the visitors at least. The pyrotechnic artistry of Torré produced amazing concoctions of fantasy and mythology. The 'Forge of Vulcan' was an oft repeated favourite, in which after the fireworks, a curtain rose to reveal Vulcan and Cyclops at the forge behind Mount Etna and the arrival of Venus with Cupid seeking arrows for her son, before the mountain spectacularly erupted, streaming lava down its sides.

A mineral spring discovered on the land added to the attractions, but the concerts were few and far between, replaced in June 1775 by the whimsical sketches of 'The Modern Magic Lantern' and a conjurer. The Forge of Vulcan was revived the following year, but despite a pretty panorama of the boulevards of Paris, with the boxes fronting the ballroom transformed into the shops of 'Newfangle the milliner', 'Trinket the toyman' and 'Crotchet the music seller', the gardens closed on 23 September 1776.

VAUXHALL (1770–1859)

There was a problem with rowdy behaviour during the 1770s, especially as it became customary to go wild on the last night of the season. As Young Branghton writes in Evelina, the last night at Vauxhall is the best: 'there is always a riot – and there the folks run about – and then there's such squalling! And there all the lamps are broke and all the women run skimper scamper.'

Opposite: From 1797 to 1835, C. H. Simpson was the Master of Ceremonies and renowned for his panache, here greeting the Duke of Wellington: 'Now Mr Simpson says that he will do his best endeavour To grant his Vauxhall friends their wish, their each delight and pleasure.'

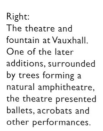

Above left: Marylebone Gardens, c.1778. The structure of the gardens remained the same but the entertainments were ever changing. In 1773 the City Surveyor discovered a mineral spring in the grounds and the Marybone Spa opened on 6 June 1774, serving the waters which would 'strengthen the stomach' from 6 a.m. each day.

Above right: Miss Ann Catley appeared at Marylebone Gardens in 1763 when she was only eighteen, and again in 1771 to sing 'Sweet Echo' from *Comus*. By this time she was principal singer at Covent Garden.

Left: *The Supper at Vauxhall* by George Cruickshank. Long tables were set out under the trees in the Grove as a more sociable contrast to the supper boxes, which would only seat six to eight guests.

Right:
The theatre and fountain at Vauxhall. One of the later additions, surrounded by trees forming a natural amphitheatre, the theatre presented ballets, acrobats and other performances.

Rowlandson's view of Vauxhall (*c.*1784) showing the orchestra with supper boxes beneath. The covered walk is behind the crowd, its painted curtains drawn up between the cast-iron pillars of the colonnade. The brightness and artificiality of the Grove is in marked contrast to the natural beauty beyond.

Jonathan Tyers's sons took over and maintained his legacy, managing Vauxhall with little change until 1792, when the entrance shilling was doubled to 2s. Tickets cost far more for the gala nights and masquerades that became hugely popular during the decade. Fireworks, which had long been a feature at Marylebone, Cuper's and Ranelagh, made an overdue debut at Vauxhall, becoming a permanent fixture from 1813. Madame Saqui appeared as the first of a new kind of entertainment as she ascended an inclined rope 350 feet long. Having reached the summit, her descent was made amid a 'tempest of fireworks'.

Ticket for the Vauxhall Jubilee, Monday 29 May 1786. The Ridotto to celebrate the approximate jubilee displayed 14,000 additional lamps to a company dressed in Dominoes as at the original Ridotto in 1732.

It was a far cry from the New Spring Gardens Pepys knew, and there were more adjustments made for Vauxhall Gardens to face the dawn of the nineteenth century.

Tom, Jerry and Logic Making the Most of an Evening at Vauxhall. Isaac and George Cruickshank captured the joy of the evening of 2 July 1821 as well as the beauty and the fashion.

35

Plan of Vauxhall Gardens (1826) showing the changes. The South Walk was stripped of its triumphal arches and renamed the Firework Walk as it led to the Firework Tower. The Cross Walk was now the Chinese Walk for its pretty Chinese lanterns.

A supper room was added next to the Rotunda in 1786, and part of the Grand Walk, with two sides of the Grove, was covered by a vaulted colonnade. Although convenient on a wet evening, it ruined what Walpole called the 'gardenhood' of the place, not least because in 1810–11 many of the trees in the Grove were cut down, taking away the last of those that survived from Tyers's day.

The 1822 season opened with a full variety programme and the new title 'The Royal Gardens, Vauxhall' in acknowledgement of the patronage of George IV in his days as Prince. The Rotunda was reinvented as an Indian Garden Room – later to be devoted to equestrian performances – whilst the adjoining saloon became the Heptaplasiesoptron with revolving pillars, palm trees climbed by twining serpents and a tinkling fountain illuminated by coloured lamps. All were in myriad repeat due to a series of glass plates that cast multiple reflections. Rope dancing took the place of the cascade that once was a defining feature of the old Vauxhall, and an exhibition of waterworks took over the Rural Downs. A Hermit's Cottage in remarkable transparency showed the hermit studying by lamplight, and four cosmoramas had replaced the ruins. The walks were changed to include a Firework Walk, a Chinese Walk with Chinese lanterns, and a new Italian Walk.

Entertainment was popularised or, as some thought, vulgarised with comic songs, but there was ballet to keep brows uplifted. Vauxhall led the way in re-enactments with the Battle of Waterloo in 1827 staged with 1,000 horse and foot soldiers. For thirty-six years C. H. Simpson was the Master of Ceremonies and one of the beloved institutions. He dressed distinctly in black silk knee breeches, frilled shirt and a coat of 'antique cut'. In his left hand he carried a tasselled, silver-headed cane, leaving his right free to raise his hat in welcome to all he met. Thackeray called him 'the gentle Simpson, that kind, smiling idiot' but Robert Cruickshank immortalised him, and a giant 45-foot effigy of him in classic welcoming stance set in coloured lamps was exhibited in the gardens from 1833.

From 1836 Vauxhall opened by day for balloon ascents, but popularity was failing fast and closure was announced in 1841. This got as far as a sale of some of the fixtures and fittings,

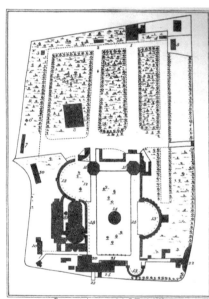

From an actual survey made by T. Allen in 1826.

VAUXHALL GARDENS.

1 Fire work Tower
2 Evening Star
3 Hermitage
4 Smugglers Cave
5 House in which M⁓ Barrett died
6 Statue of Milton
7 Transparency
8 Theatre
9 Chinese entrance
10 Artificers work shops
11 Octagon temples
12 Fountain
13 Circles of Boxes
14 Orchestra
15 Collonade
16 Rotunda
17 Picture Room
18 Supper Room
19 Ice House
20 Bar
21 Princes Pavillion
22 Entrance
23 Water Gate
24 House

including twenty-four of Hayman's supper box paintings, before reprieve. A new programme of entertainments and masquerades and the conversion of the oil lamps to gas helped to maintain interest, but the removal of the orchestra's traditional cocked hats boded poorly. The final years of the 1850s were marred by constant complaints about the *bals masqués*, which continued until 6 am and attracted 'disreputable characters'.

The final concert was held on Monday 25 July 1859 with equestrian performances and one last firework display. There was an auction the following month where Edward Tyrrell Smith bought the remaining supper box paintings for the banqueting hall at his new Pleasure Garden, Cremorne, and by 1864 Vauxhall's 12 acres were built upon.

Above left: Balloon Ascent at Vauxhall Gardens in 1849 – these ascents were a popular part of the daytime programme but many, such as 'Boz', felt that Vauxhall without night's cloak of illusion was like 'a porter-pot without the porter'

Above: The New Ballet at Vauxhall, July 1852 – *Zelita* or *The Maid of Calabria* was a love story feted for its 'ingeniously composed pas, much graceful grouping, picturesque costumes and pretty scenery'.

Left: Vauxhall in *Punch*, 1850 – finally, as fortunes failed and the 'last night' at Vauxhall was announced one too many times, Vauxhall became a pastiche.

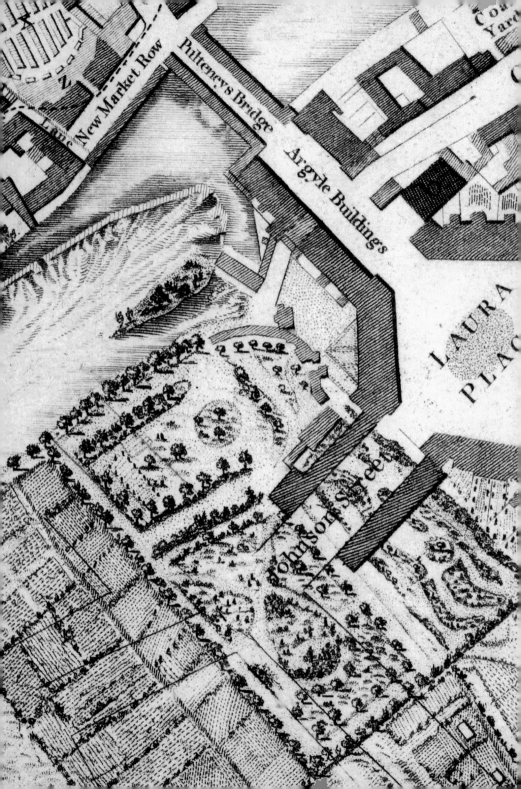

EIGHTEENTH-CENTURY PROVINCIAL GARDENS

So MANY HISTORIES concentrate on London, giving the impression that there was a cultural void outside of the city, but most towns were not without a Pleasure Garden of some sort. Although considerable ingenuity went into the design and laying out of many beautiful spaces, the same cannot be said of the naming of them: the same names – Spring Gardens, Ranelagh and Vauxhall – were used time and again all over the country. What is confusing to us now was then a rather successful marketing exercise, each garden claiming something of the status of its great London namesake.

NORWICH

Norwich was a powerful city, in a prime location to access mainland Europe; before the railway arrived in 1845 it was quicker to reach Amsterdam by boat than London by road. The Pleasure Garden must have hit a particular note of accord in Norfolk as for many years there were four Pleasure Gardens in competition.

My Lord's Garden, first built in 1663, extended down to the banks of the river Wensum at Cunsford. It was a low-key success, serving 'good liquors and fruits' until William Curtis took the lease in 1770, adding the increasingly popular firework demonstrations. He also made more radical improvements, building a pretty shell-work grotto and displaying a series of views including the Cathedral in Florence, the Quirinal in Rome and the London Ranelagh Gardens. He added an artificial cascade based on the famous one at Vauxhall, judging his to be better as it had swans on the water. More amazing mechanical concoctions followed, including a sea-flight with five ships, the storming of a castle, and a view of Vesuvius. It is unclear at what point My Lord's Garden ceased to attract visitors, but the last mention of it is for a fantastical firework display in 1775.

The gardener John Moore was inspired by New Spring Gardens in London, and in 1739 opened his own of the same name 200 yards upstream from My Lord's Garden. Not unlike the original, it was an idyllic rural retreat where visitors would enjoy the river views and relax whilst drinking and dining in the shady bowers accompanied by birdsong.

Opposite:
Detail from the Harcourt Masters Map of Bath 1808, showing Spring Gardens (courtesy of www.bathintime. co.uk – Bath Central Library). Spring Gardens is off Johnson Street to the left of Laura Place; its later design is more Romantic than Harrison's Walks and less formal.

Merry-making, with a view of Norwich, from Richmond Hill Gardens by Robert Ladbrooke, *c.*1816 (courtesy of Norwich Castle Museum and Art Gallery). The only surviving depiction of any of the Norwich Pleasure Gardens, it shows the delight taken in impromptu music (from the musicians behind the dancers) and good ale!

Nestling close to the remnants of the medieval city walls near Ber Street Gates was the Wilderness. Aside from being laid out in groves of trees by Samuel Bruister in 1748, little is known of the Wilderness until 1768, when it hosted illuminated evening concerts and experimented in public breakfasting. In 1773 lamps and fireworks were added, and the old Long Walk under the city wall was re-gravelled in preparation for Assize Week, when cotillions and country dances were added to the programme. Competition between the gardens was fierce, and during the 1775 season, as well as many pyrotechnical delights, the Wilderness boasted amongst its attractions mechanical devices that would stun any audience, including a distant waterfall, a working watermill, sheep, swans and a heron!

The last of the quartet was Smith's Rural Gardens, opened in 1766. Designed to be a cut above, security was provided at the illuminated grounds 'to keep out such persons as may be thought disagreeable'. There were fireworks and a Grand Walk 'with lights fixed to the tables in a new taste', and, faithful to its roots as a nursery garden, the grounds were glorious with flowers. During Assize Week entrance was a shilling, 8d of which was redeemable in fruit and the Herefordshire cider or Westall's fine nog that was served. In 1772 the pyrotechnician Quantrell took over, his stunning displays in the style of Marylebone's Torré proving incredibly successful. In 1775, aided by Torré's former assistant, they revived the Vulcan's Forge and eruption of Mount Etna motif, this time staging it within a huge 21-foot globe, which revolved around its axis before falling into quarters to reveal the scene.

In 1776 James Bunn, the artist and scenery painter for Norwich Theatre, took over New Spring Garden, using his talents to great effect and exhibiting a series of his own paintings. He added a rotunda styled after the Pantheon in Oxford Street, which could seat a thousand, and later imported the artificial waterfall that had been at the Wilderness. Increasing competition between Bunn and Quantrell inspired ever more incredible firework displays, but unfortunately it ended badly in 1782 when an explosion killed a man. Bunn managed to beat Quantrell and exhibited the first hot air balloon in Norwich at the Pantheon in New Spring Garden in 1784, only for Quantrell to go one better the following year by holding the first manned balloon ascent.

In 1794 New Spring Gardens was aggrandised and renamed Vauxhall. Continuing in the rivalrous spirit, in 1797 the Rural Gardens was re-christened Ranelagh by new owner Neech, who made various improvements making use of fixtures from the defunct Vauxhall to create a large 2,000-seat Amphitheatre. The Saloon served jelly and ices and was newly adorned with twenty picturesque and romantic views. There were three bars serving refreshments, and the new Chinese Walks were festooned with lanterns.

Part of the gardens at the western end of the Wilderness was re-opened in about 1812 primarily for fireworks and renamed as Richmond Hill Gardens. In 1827 part of the medieval wall collapsed, and the writers of *The Annals of Norwich* criticised the proprietor for detracting from 'the romantic beauty attached to these grounds' by replacing it with a screen. In the 1840s houses were built and the gardens became private, but part of the wall and the accompanying wall walk still remain.

The Dance (1782) by F. Bartolozzi after H.W. Bunbury. Dancing was always important, not only for sheer pleasure, but as a rare and convivial way to get close to the opposite sex.

Music *al fresco* was often quite formal.

In 1842 Ranelagh became the Victoria Gardens and the emphasis of the entertainments became focused on pantomime, Romantic drama and ballet whilst, rather ironically, the new gardens springing up were decidedly rustic, echoing those of the previous century. Tragic decline was curling the once gilded edges, and in 1849 Victoria Gardens was sold. Where the railways were indirectly responsible for most Pleasure Garden closures, here it was more literal, as Victoria Gardens became Victoria Station, the Saloon becoming the waiting rooms, and the Amphitheatre becoming the ticket office and luggage room.

BATH

The spa towns had a tradition of formal walks dating back to the 1630s, as exercise was often prescribed along with such vast quantities of the water that visitors must have been sloshing at every pace! Bath, the ultimate spa, had been a resort even in Roman days when fallen legionaries were brought there to recover under the auspices of Minerva. It was enjoyed by royalty from Elizabeth I to James II, yet it still retained its easy, frivolous air – possibly because the mixed bathing was usually naked!

Laid out at the beginning of the eighteenth century, Harrison's Walks, or the Gravel Walks, was a popular place for promenading. There was a card room, tearoom, and a ballroom added in 1720, before the name was changed to the Orange Grove in honour of William of Orange who visited in 1734.

Parade Gardens and Harrison's Walks. Fan view c.1752–3 (courtesy of www.bathintime.co.uk – Private Collection). Also known as the Gravel Walks, they were the first Pleasure Gardens in Bath.

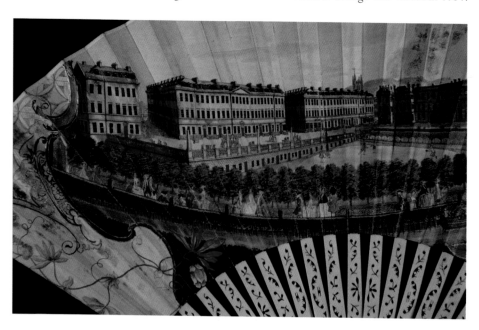

Fan view of Harrison's Walks, 1749 (courtesy of www.bathintime.co.uk – Private Collection). Beau Nash, the 'uncrowned King of Bath' and his party are depicted enjoying a promenade by the river Avon.

Public breakfasting with music was popular at Spring Gardens: opened in the 1730s, it was accessed by water until the Pulteney Bridge was opened in 1774. Both of these venues were small, allowing plenty of opportunity to be recognised, bowed to and acknowledged as part of genteel society. This was a 'must' at a time when many, including Jane Austen, observed that Bath, now packed with nouveaux riches, was becoming an over-fashionable parody of itself.

LIVERPOOL

The burgeoning cities also had their share of Pleasure Gardens. Although Liverpool has its own Vauxhall area near the Leeds and Liverpool Canal, it was on the site that is now the Adelphi Hotel (built in 1826) where Ranelagh Gardens once stood. Opened in 1759 behind the White-House Tavern,

The Montgolfier Balloon. From the moment that the Montgolfier brothers made their first successful hot air balloon ascent, bright balloon silks became ubiquitous in the skies above England's Pleasure Gardens.

Detail from George Perry's 1769 map of Liverpool showing Ranelagh Gardens (Courtesy of Liverpool Record Office) – the elegant formal space in intriguing contrast to the rope walks nearby.

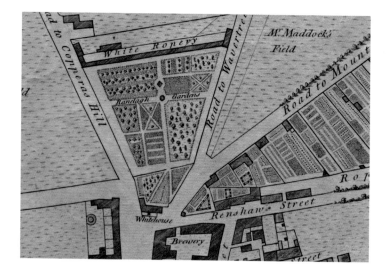

sometimes known as Ranelagh House, the gardens were laid out with seats, an orchestra for concerts and recitals, and there was the occasional firework display 'in the Vauxhall style'. During the 1790s there was a Chinese concert room, and the gardens, lush with strawberries, were very popular during the fruiting season. It is not recorded why popularity waned, but Ranelagh Gardens were no longer entertaining the public by the end of the eighteenth century.

Liverpool also had the Spring Garden tea gardens and the Folly Gardens, which closed in 1785. The curious Mount Zion was a public esplanade that descended the hill overlooking what was once a quarry and then a classically ornate cemetery with Grecian-style chapel and catacombs. The Mayor had it laid out as a work creation project to occupy the unemployed poor during a hard winter, but it caused a scandal when a local clergyman objected to the notice that announced the sale of bottled beer in juxtaposition to such a holy name. It was still in existence in 1842, although it was renamed St James's Walk.

NEWCASTLE UPON TYNE

Newcastle upon Tyne was served by two gardens in the eighteenth century, New Ranelagh Gardens and New Spring Gardens just outside the city walls to the west. The *Newcastle Courant* gives notice in June 1760 of the opening of a public garden near the town, known as the New Ranelagh Gardens, 'with a concert of music and other entertainments for the season'. In 1763 the New Spring Gardens became known for their concerts, held weekly during the summer months over several years. It was still marked as 'Gardens' in

Oliver's map of Newcastle in 1844, but had been replaced by the Spring Garden Ironworks by 1878. As well as music, the city enjoyed its share of balloon ascents and other amusements, which were probably also held at the gardens.

BIRMINGHAM

Despite being little more than a scattering of villages prior to the Industrial Revolution, Birmingham had a variety of public gardens. There was a garden at Deritend, and from the middle of the eighteenth century Bridgeman's Apollo Gardens at Aston hosted concerts.

The first advertisements for entertainments at the Vauxhall Gardens at Duddeston Hall appeared in 1738. Initially this largely consisted of cockfights, but thankfully by the 1750s tastes were more salubrious. By the 1790s it was immensely popular and renowned as 'a pleasant retreat with its bright parterres, its numerous gravel walks bordered by lofty trees, its bowling green, orchestra, and other attractions'. The nineteenth century brought even greater successes, adding glittering illuminations and balloon ascents to their repertoire of events accompanied by 'fine wines and viands'. By the 1830s, as Birmingham expanded, Vauxhall became less fashionable, but it still managed to attract some of the more popular performers from London. Finally the railway built right up to the boundary wall, and the ravenous expansion of the city demanded Vauxhall as a sacrifice and a final farewell ball was held on 16 September 1850.

Vauxhall Gardens at Duddeston (courtesy of Birmingham Museums and Art Galleries). The gardens were so beloved that a painting was made to commemorate their passing in 1850, and for many years it was displayed in the window of the Victoria Building Society, Union Street.

NINETEENTH-CENTURY
PROVINCIAL GARDENS

Fashionable ball gown (1824), worn with delicate dancing slippers, which, as they could be seen beneath the skirt, were swapped from foot to foot to preserve their straight shape despite discomfort to the wearer.

ONCE the Napoleonic Wars were over, England got on with the business of prosperity. In the 1830s, Budding's lawnmower revolutionised gardening, allowing even small-scale middle-class gardeners to have a lawn without the need for sheep, or scores of scythe-wielding servants to trim it. A repeal in the tax on bricks in 1850 inspired a spate of new building, whilst the wonders of the Crystal Palace coupled with the repeal of the window tax in 1851 meant that a glasshouse was the latest 'must have' accessory. Finally, the repeal of the paper tax in 1861 helped to cultivate a huge new crop of gardening journals that disseminated new ideas on a weekly basis, making the collection of rare exotic plants, especially orchids and chrysanthemums, increasingly competitive.

The Victorians tackled their gardens with the same fervour and eclectic zeal as they did most things. No corner of the world, modern or ancient, or annal of history was left unturned in pursuit of inspiration, and everything was interpreted in the boldest and brightest sense possible. Repton had used flowers as a feature on his pretty balustraded terraces, and bright splashes of colour were sometimes rather garishly reintroduced. The greenhouse made it possible for vast numbers of tender annuals to be raised and used en masse in the bright carpet bedding that became popular at Cremorne and remains a feature of public parks today. Discarded over a century earlier, topiary was brought back to add spectacular architectural features.

BATH: SYDNEY GARDENS VAUXHALL (1795–c.1845)

At last visitors to England's most elegant town could indulge in the pleasures of their city cousins. Planned by the architect Baldwin as the main feature to the Pulteney Estate, spanning 12 acres, Sydney Gardens was the largest Pleasure Garden outside London. The hexagonal gardens were entered via the Sydney Hotel with its superb pedimented portico and Corinthian columns offering a gracious welcome. Behind this, there was a large semicircular balcony (which could accommodate a hundred-piece orchestra) supported by Ionic

Sydney Gardens c.1804. Classic view of the rear of the Sydney Hotel, showing the orchestra above the transparency of Apollo with his lyre.

columns. Imported from the beleaguered Apollo Gardens – which flanked Westminster Bridge until troublesome pickpockets caused it to be closed in 1793 – the loggia below the orchestra featured a backlit transparency of Apollo with his lyre, affording a magical hint of the pleasures that lay beyond.

Twin semicircular sweeps of supper boxes trailed off to each side of the hotel, providing outside dining in addition to the tearooms, card room and ballroom within. Accessed by the elegant tree-lined walks decorated with variegated lamps amongst the thatched pavilions, the delights within included grottoes, waterfalls and two Chinese-style iron bridges built over the canal.

Sydney House From The Garden, c.1815 (courtesy of www.bathintime.co.uk Bath Central Library). Sydney Gardens were in their heyday with the orchestra in full swing and every supper box crowded.

The Labyrinth in Sydney Gardens (courtesy of www.bathintime.co.uk - Bath Central Library). View of the labyrinth with the route to Merlin's Swings mapped out by a dotted line.

The Labyrinth in Sydney Gardens, Bath.
The dotted line denotes the path to be pursued

The bandstand in Sydney Gardens, c.1870. By the Victorian era the musical focus of the gardens had been moved away from the balcony to the heart of the gardens.

Romantic sensibilities ran wild with a faux ruined castle complete with cannon, but it was the labyrinth that was Jane Austen's favourite, as she proclaimed when moving to 4 Sydney Place in 1801: 'It would be very pleasant to be near the Sydney Gardens. We could go into the labyrinth every day.'

As with the London Vauxhall Gardens, Sydney Gardens continued to provide exceptional entertainments until the late 1840s, but its elegant heyday as a Pleasure Garden was over when Jane Austen's beloved labyrinth was destroyed by the incursion of Brunel's Great Western Railway.

MANCHESTER: TINKER'S GARDENS (1797–1852)

There was a Spring Gardens in Manchester before 1729 in what was later Fountain Street, but it was the end of the eighteenth century before Robert Tinker (1766–1836) took charge of the city's outdoor entertainments. *Scholes' Directory* for 1797 notes Tinker as proprietor of the Grape & Compass Coffee House and Tea Gardens at Collyhurst, but he clearly saw the potential of the lovely spot leading down to the river Irk and gained a victualler's licence, renaming it the Elysian Gardens.

The gardens were adorned with 3,000 coloured lights, transforming it into an Elysian retreat. There were singers in addition to the usual band, and the evening was promised to be 'at once intellectual, rural, and delightful', all for the 1s. 6d entrance fee!

In 1814 the name was changed again to Vauxhall Gardens, but beloved by the locals, it had been christened and remained Tinker's Gardens. Less formal than its London counterpart, there was dancing on the lawns, and refreshments were served at tables under verdant festoons from the overhanging trees or in lush leafy bowers. Clearly the land was prodigiously fecund, as in 1814 a notice was issued:

> 'To the Admirers of Cucumbers – At these Gardens may be seen, a CUCUMBER, which measures seven feet, eight inches long. One from the same plant was sent for the Prince Regent's inspection. It is allowed by all gardeners and others who have seen it, to be the greatest curiosity of its kind Nature ever produced in this kingdom.'

The spectacular Belle Vue Gardens were primarily zoological gardens, but after the opening of Longsight Station gave a major boost to visitor numbers it became a Manchester institution, the zoo at least remaining open until the late 1970s.

There were other attractions, including the ever-popular balloon ascent. An advertisement from August 1827 announces the Royal Coronation Balloon Ascent, stating the gardens 'are so happily disposed by nature as to form a complete amphitheatre' to afford 'uninterrupted observance of every preliminary preparation'.

Robert Tinker died in 1836 but the gardens continued until 1852, albeit with less sparkle and increasing competition from Belle Vue Zoological Gardens, which opened in 1837.

ROYAL LEAMINGTON SPA: RANELAGH GARDENS (1811–c.1849)

The first baths at the Spa of Leamington Priors were opened in 1786. Dr Lambe's pamphlet extolled its virtues in 1794, saying it was 'likely to cast Bath and every other Spa into the shade', and the illustrious visitors started to arrive, including three duchesses in one season. They needed to be entertained, and in 1811 Mackie established Leamington Nursery and Pleasure Grounds, later to become known as Ranelagh Gardens. It covered 10 acres consisting of 'Beautiful public walks, Shrubberies, fruit and flowers...' There were gala nights with music, fireworks and Montgolfier balloons throughout the 1820s.

The Eagle Foundry was built nearby in 1833, and as it prospered, it

The Royal Pump Room was opened in 1814 when gardens and walks were laid out to provide pleasant promenades and evening concerts for their patrons. The gardens were opened to the public in 1875.

encroached ever closer to Ranelagh Gardens. This was probably the reason why the gardens were enclosed by a high wall in the 1840s. As development began on the other side of the river, the town shifted its focus north to the 'new town'. Fully eclipsed by Jephson Gardens, which opened opposite the Royal Pump Rooms in 1846, Ranelagh reverted to its original purpose as a nursery and was auctioned off in 1849.

Jephson Gardens were dedicated to Dr Jephson in 1846, and a temple housing a marble statue to him was added in 1849 – despite him being alive and well and chairing the gardens' committee. It offered all the usual entertainments, and from 1878 it hosted lawn tennis tournaments to rival those at Wimbledon.

BOSTON, LINCOLNSHIRE: VAUXHALL GARDENS (1815–c.1830s)

Designed on 2 acres by Charles Cave in 1813, this was far smaller than the others with Vauxhall pretensions. It opened in 1815 and ten years later a maze, a marine grotto and a Cosmorama were added.

In 1829 the gardens opened for the season on 1 May, with new views of York Cathedral amongst those that could be viewed at the Cosmorama. At the Grand Gala on 12 August country dancing in the Saloon was an added feature. The following year, 'In Commemoration of His Majesty's Birth Day... considerable alterations have been made in the Promenade Department since last season, which will be lighted up with Variegated Lamps and Transparencies.'

One can assume that these new features were very costly, as admittance to the gardens and maze at 6d in 1829 had risen to 2s. in 1830.

THE VICTORIAN
PLEASURE GARDENS

CREMORNE GARDENS

Just when the popularity of the Royal Vauxhall Gardens was finally starting to wane, Cremorne began to make its ascent. An attractive villa on the river at Chelsea, it was built by the ninth Earl of Huntingdon in 1740 for his pious Methodist wife, and known as Chelsea Farm until it became the home of the Viscount of Cremorne. Bought by Baron Charles de Berenger in 1830, he saw its potential as a resort and built a 'stadium' where young men could indulge in the manly pursuits of swimming, rowing, shooting and fencing.

It had expanded its facilities and its popularity by the end of the decade, and when up for sale in 1840, it was described as 'a splendid place of entertainment', which could rival Vauxhall Gardens if managed by 'a spirited individual with a moderate capital and a well furnished head'. Maybe Renton Nicholson considered himself to be such, as Cremorne was in his hands by 1843. 'Baron' Nicholson presided over the scandalous, sometimes indecent mock trials of the infamous Judge and Jury Society in Bow Street, and it was suggested that he had imported the society to Cremorne. In 1846 he did import his business partner from the Garrick's Head, Thomas Bartlett Simpson, whose inspired entertainments made the gardens a roaring success.

They had already had success with such fascinating acts as 'Burke's celebrated pony Bobby', who could 'trot seven miles and a half in thirty minutes with a monkey on his back', and now added some more permanent features. Reflecting the modern taste for sport, by 1867 the gardens were crowded with diversions, including a marionette theatre, a circus, a shooting gallery, an American bowling saloon and a diorama. There were still opportunities to sample the more traditional Pleasure Garden features of viewing the Hermit's Cave – now interactive, as the hermit 'of celebrated prophetic knowledge' would tell the future. There was also a Gypsy Grotto and a 'monster oyster-shell grotto', where the air was scented 'most appropriately with Rummell's Sea-weed Bouquet' and where seafood was served by 'young ladies dressed as mermaids'! There were fountains and an attractive fernery, and horticultural exhibitions were held at Ashburnham Hall.

Opposite:
The Medieval Tournament at Cremorne. Some years previously Lord Eglington's tournament had been ruined by an inopportune cloudburst forcing the Black Knight to put a mackintosh over his armour, so, just in case, the tournament was staged in the adjacent Ashburnham Pavilion.

As the *Illustrated London News* reported, there were 'Lavender bowers, Chinese walks, trees illuminated with jets of gas, and flower-beds glittering with coloured lamps'. A gorgeous grand pagoda filled with an orchestra of fifty presided over 'a vast circle or plateau for the votaries of Terpsichore' that was able to accommodate 4,000 dancers. On many nights it was full to capacity by 8.30 pm. Many of the more genteel visitors would opt for supper served at Cremorne House for half a crown first, and arrive on the dance floor at 11 pm when it was quieter.

Those wanting a little more solitude could venture into the maze, which provided a romantic walk during the day but a far more seamy experience late in the evening, when it was to the abundance of prostitutes what the infamous Dark Walk at Vauxhall was to the strumpets of earlier centuries.

In August 1858 there was maypole dancing and morris dancing, Hugo Vamp's singing and dancing marionettes, and the *Cirque Orientale* with 'equestrians of every nation and clowns of every clime'. Generally, though, the entertainments were becoming ever more spectacular, and at times quite bizarre! The *Illustrated London News* reported in September 1858 on the 'Italian Salamander' Cristofero Buono Core and his experiment to prove his 'dress was impervious to fire and will preserve the body though in contact with flame': two intersecting corridors of brushwood 7 feet high and 3 feet wide were set ablaze, and whilst the crowd 30 feet away were scorched from the blaze, he passed through unscathed! Although somewhat less spectacular than the 1826 performance of the fire-eater Chabert (who consumed arsenic and

Cremorne Gardens (1864) by Phoebus Levin (courtesy of Bridgeman Art Library). Enclosed with ornamental ironwork and adorned with garnet and emerald glass, the dancing platform was spectacular with the light of the huge gas-lit chandeliers.

boiling oil before entering a huge oven and cooking a leg of lamb which he then served to his audience), Core was a veteran of the Napoleonic Wars and had a scientific interest in developing fire-retardant clothing.

Battle re-enactments had been popular since the Battle of Waterloo staged at Vauxhall in 1827, and the 1851 Naval Fête went with a huge bang when the hull of an ancient steamer, filled with explosive material, was the climax of the naval battle when it caught fire, burning pieces hurling into the air to settle on the river with a hiss. A medieval tournament provided a somewhat safer

Cremorne Gardens (c.1877) by James McNeill Whistler (courtesy of David Coke). Whistler lived during the 1870s in Cheyne Walk just a few hundred yards away from Cremorne and made a series of paintings of the nightlife there, this one reminiscent of a scene at Montmartre.

The maypole dance at Cremorne, 9 July 1858 – after two hundred years, maypole and morris dancing were still popular at the Pleasure Gardens!

The Italian Salamander at Cremorne Gardens – one of the more sensational animal-themed entertainments offered along with Natator the 'Man-Frog' who ate, smoked and slept in a tank of water, and Signor Devani the 'Orang-utan Contortionist'.

spectacle in July 1863, when the *Illustrated London News* was hugely impressed by the stunning display, costumes and weaponry of the procession but found the lengthy duration and the lack of variety in the combat monotonous.

Technology was frequently applied to entertainment, allowing for all kinds of spectacle and illusion. The Diorama had become popular in the 1820s, a theatrical experience whereby audiences viewed a remarkably realistic scene exquisitely painted on multilayered fine linen roll past on a loop. Sometimes audience members were revolved slowly on a huge turntable to give the effect of travelling through the scene. This was the

The Female Blondin: Madame Genevieve Young crossed on a tightrope 100 feet above the Thames at Cremorne. As she reached the middle she nearly fell, as the rope suddenly went slack when some unscrupulous spectator stole the lead weights for the guy ropes!

principle applied to the Stereorama, new for the season of 1860, which conveyed the experience of travelling through the Gotthard Pass into Italy.

Aside from the usual balloon ascents, the 'Flying Man' Vincent de Groof attempted to go one better and launch his bat-like flying machine from a platform suspended from a hot air balloon high above the crowd. Tragically, his faith in the contraption with its vast 37-foot wingspan and 18-foot tail was misplaced, and a sudden gust of wind caused him to plummet to his death. He was not the first performer to die at Cremorne: Carlo de Valeria had taken a fatal fall from his tightrope eleven years before in 1863.

Cremorne Gardens gathered an increasingly unsavoury reputation for rowdiness and vandalism; the pavilions and bars were damaged and local residents were kept awake late at night. There were even more complaints about the 'Fulham virgins' who plied the oldest trade at the gates on the King's Road, and Cremorne was eventually condemned as 'a nursery of every kind of vice' in a defamatory pamphlet. Forced to bring a libel suit against its author, a local Baptist minister, the proprietor John Baum finally won his case in 1877, but, with damages of only a farthing against crippling costs, he was forced to close. After a sale of everything including the famous dance floor in 1878, the entire site save for the King's Road gates was demolished in 1880.

SURREY GARDENS (1836–78)

The Surrey Gardens began life as Surrey Zoological Gardens in 1836, but, not content to be limited to animals, they also hosted a slew of other events. Their panoramas were legendary, offering a sterling mix of patriotism and pyrotechnics, including a Vesuvius with firework eruptions, the Great Fire of London, the Siege of Gibraltar and the Storming of Badajoz.

They also offered the ubiquitous balloon ascent, but with a zoological twist. Signor Jacopo, a tiny monkey dressed in scarlet coat and feathers, was sent up in the balloon and made a parachute descent over Walworth Common, and a prize of £2 was offered for the first person to find him! The vast Montgolfier balloon caused more problems when it caught fire. When the ascent was abandoned, the more obstreperous members of the disappointed 5,000-strong crowd stoned the balloon and smashed all the windows of the conservatory that was the lion enclosure.

The huge glasshouses that held the menagerie were rather overshadowed by the advent of the Crystal Palace built for the Great Exhibition in 1851, and the animals were

The zoological flavour persisted at the gardens and the poor Indian tortoise was still giving rides to children in 1852, despite being over two hundred years old.

The new face of Surrey Gardens, 19 July 1856, a year after the giant 12,000-seat Lake Music Hall was built.

sold off in 1855. An enormous 12,000-seat music hall was built next to the magnificent lake, and Surrey Gardens had a change of heart as well as a change of management. For a few years the vast hall attracted the finest variety acts and resounded each Sunday to the sermons of popular minister C. H. Spurgeon. But fortunes were blighted by a fatal accident in 1856, when seven people died during a hoax fire alarm, and when (somewhat ironically) the music hall was destroyed by fire in 1861, it was not rebuilt, but replaced by a theatre offering Cremorne-style light entertainments. After temporarily housing St Thomas's Hospital whilst it moved premises, it was closed in 1878. Surrey Gardens had been superseded, and like so many Pleasure Gardens, its prime land had become more valuable to the Victorian property boom than as public space.

The Siege of Gibraltar was one of the stunning firework extravaganzas staged; the reflections from the lake added another dimension to the drama.

Rosherville Gardens (1841). The aura of the disused quarry is still quite discernible although it is clear that its new pretty design is growing in.

ROSHERVILLE GARDENS, GRAVESEND (1837–c.1914)

Londoners had always enjoyed the opportunity to take to the river to leave the confines of the city. As the Victorian era got under way they wanted to go further, and Rosherville Gardens in Gravesend were the ideal day-tripping distance.

The battlemented tower heralded Rosherville's presence to those arriving by river, and presided over 18 acres which included a maze, a museum, a 'baronial hall' for dancing and refreshments, a concert room, a fortune-telling gypsy in her tent, a fernery, a bear-pit and miles of walks.

Rosherville truly was 'The Place to spend a Happy Day' that the posters promised – that is until 3 September 1878, the day of the *Princess Alice* disaster. The passenger steamer was returning to Swan Pier near London Bridge that warm summer's evening, heavily laden with passengers, when there was a horrendous collision with a much larger vessel. The *Princess Alice* sank in less than four minutes, killing more than 640 people including more than 200 children. Local legend has it that the Reach is still haunted by the captain desperately searching for those who were never found.

Unusually, the advent of the railway in May 1886 actually helped Rosherville's popularity, bringing up to 20,000 passengers a week from London directly to a dedicated Rosherville station. Despite problems with drunken visitors, foul weather and financial issues, entertainments continued with only the odd hiatus until 1907. There was a renaissance at Rosherville in 1909 when Edward Swift took over, making the gardens sparkle with electric lamps and red gravel in the flowerbeds, and revamping the zoo with baby elephant Kim offering children rides. Scandal hit when Swift was accused of stealing a cashbox, and despite crowds cheering at his acquittal, the gardens were closed again in 1911.

THE ROSE OF ROSHERVILLE

BALLAD.

SUNG BY MISS AMELIA SESTINI.

WRITTEN AND COMPOSED
BY
WILLIAM WILSON

BY THE SAME COMPOSER
THE ROSHERVILLE WALTZ 4/-
THE ROSHERVILLE GALOP 4/-

THOˢ W LEE LITH GROSVENOR MEWS BOND STᵂ

ARCADIA FALLEN

WHERE George III had enjoyed the delights of the Pleasure Gardens, wishing to evade the constraints of his father's court, George IV drew everyone who was anyone with him to the fantastical Pavilion in Brighton. Left to society's newest group, the burgeoning middle classes, by the mid nineteenth century the notion of the gardens as an Arcadian retreat for the fashionable elite had largely disappeared. The scrutiny of daylight had done away with the delicate props and illusions of Tyers's day as the gardens led a dual life. In the daytime it catered to families as a sort of forerunner to the amusement park, whilst in the evenings the noise of the firework displays was rivalled only by the rowdy behaviour and vandalism fuelled by the many bars dotted around the grounds. Where once young ladies promenaded with their swains, flash young men with full wage packets came in search of the euphemistically named 'Fulham virgins', the professional and sometimes amateur ladies of the night who now dominated the scene.

The canals and railways binding the wildness of the countryside brought the inexorable message that times had changed. It was no longer enough to go across the river to get out of the city, as city and horizons had expanded. Fashionable Victorians wanted the latest 'must have', an annual family seaside holiday, whilst for consumptives, invalids and the health conscious, doctors unanimously prescribed a bracing dose of smog-free sea air.

The seaside became what the Pleasure Gardens had been in microcosm – a hedonistic getaway. Comus was exiled, and now Neptune presided; only glorious nature remained constant as its theatre. Wafer-thin ham was exchanged for oyster suppers and penny licks, 'feathered minstrels' exchanged for the *clamor nauticus* or brass bands, and the shady walks for the bright and breezy pier or promenade. The spirit of the spa remained, albeit now with salt water being advocated for both immersion and infusion, with donkey rides, tennis and cricket substituted for bowls. Most seaside towns had gardens with vivid floral displays and bandstands, and many had winter gardens offering a refuge from foul weather.

Opposite:
'The Rose of Rosherville' (sheet music, 1868, courtesy of Gravesend Library). Like Vauxhall in its day, Rosherville was so popular that it was immortalised in song. There was also a 'Rosherville Polka' and a 'Rosherville Waltz'.

Rosherville main entrance, c.1900. Visitors could pay a penny to go up the Watch Tower to look at the view, stopping off on the way up to visit the mummy of a Peruvian woman exhibited there between 1846 and the late 1870s, by which time one of her arms had fallen off.

The Promenade at Brighton. From the early 1820s the promenade offered a significant challenge to the Pleasure Gardens.

The Romantic ideals and cultural eclecticism that were the hallmark of the great Pleasure Gardens had been increasingly overshadowed by the glitzy novelty of Victorian innovation, as fashion had reversed to become a means to display wealth rather than taste. The music and performance that had been nurtured by the gardens were available at seaside theatres, music halls and assembly rooms, but the joys of art and architecture had seemingly been forgotten. Also forgotten was any egalitarian sense of a

The Steine Gardens, Brighton. The public gardens offered little diversion aside from the opportunity to promenade in royal proximity near the Royal Pavilion on its north-west side.

sharing of space, and the huge numbers of trains that set out from the cities crammed with holidaymakers still had them neatly divided into three classes.

Waiting for the excursion train: although subdivided into classes on the train the waiting crowds were jostled cheek by jowl.

INDEX